Maggie and Maddy
Adventures in Napa Valley

Written by Kyle and Amy Goleno
Illustrated by Peter Francis

ISBN 978-0-615-65199-6

Published by Maggie and Maddy Children's Books
Napa, CA USA
www.maggieandmaddy.com

Second printing | Printed in China

Illustrations by Peter Francis
Edited by Laura Peetoom
Design by Marcy Claman

Produced by Callawind Children's Books
3551 St. Charles Boulevard, Suite 179
Kirkland, Quebec H9H 3C4
www.callawind.com

To our daughters, Meghan and Katelin.
You fill our life with laughter, joy and tremendous love.

I am Maggie and I love a little adventure.
Maddy is my little sister and we do everything
together. Mom said it's my job as her big
sister to teach her and show her new things.
She didn't exactly say how I should do it.

At our age, transportation is a little hard to come by. It's lucky for us that hot air balloons fly over our backyard every morning. Today one has landed at the park across the street. This is a perfect way for us to explore Napa Valley.

"Maddy, are you ready?" I ask.
Maddy squeals, "I am so excited!"

A little hot air and up, up and away we go!

We float over the hills through the fog. Maddy thinks we are floating in a valley of fluffy marshmallows.

We made it to Calistoga.
We can see Old Faithful Geyser.
It is so cool to see water shoot
out of the ground all by itself.

Castello di Amorosa, the castle of love!

Maddy loves to dress up like a princess.
She never goes anywhere without her
crown.

This castle is big enough
for *two* princesses.

There's the trail. A little bit further into town and we can find a safe place to land.

"Maddy, please turn off all electronic devices and secure your items in your purse for landing."

Silverado Trail

That was fun. Maddy and I are starving.
Our pink bike will get us there quickly.

Mom says breakfast is the most important meal of the day. Dad always says donuts are the perfect food group. Mom says she hasn't seen any scientific research to support that, but Dad's pretty smart.

Maddy and I think these donuts are dee-licious, especially with chocolate milk. Now it's time to accessorize, and I know just the place.

So many toys, so little time! Maddy looks fabulous.
I have taught her well.

After all that shopping, this fresh air is perfect. Dad taught me how to paddle in Lake Tahoe when I was little. Now it's my turn to teach Maddy.

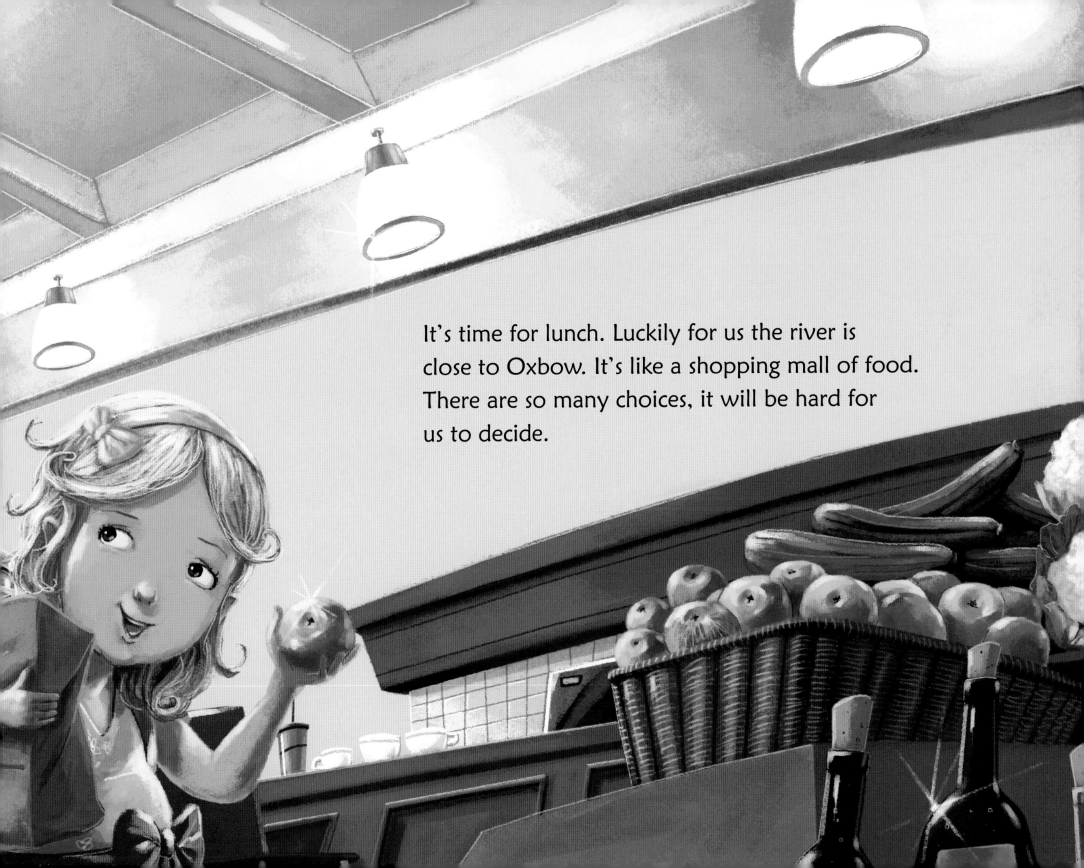

It's time for lunch. Luckily for us the river is close to Oxbow. It's like a shopping mall of food. There are so many choices, it will be hard for us to decide.

I think we made a good choice with
the mini corn dogs, fries and milkshakes.
Napa has fine food even for us kids.

Our adventure continues, by air, land, water
and now by TRAIN. Chugga-chugga, whoo whoo!
Next stop, The Culinary Institute of America.

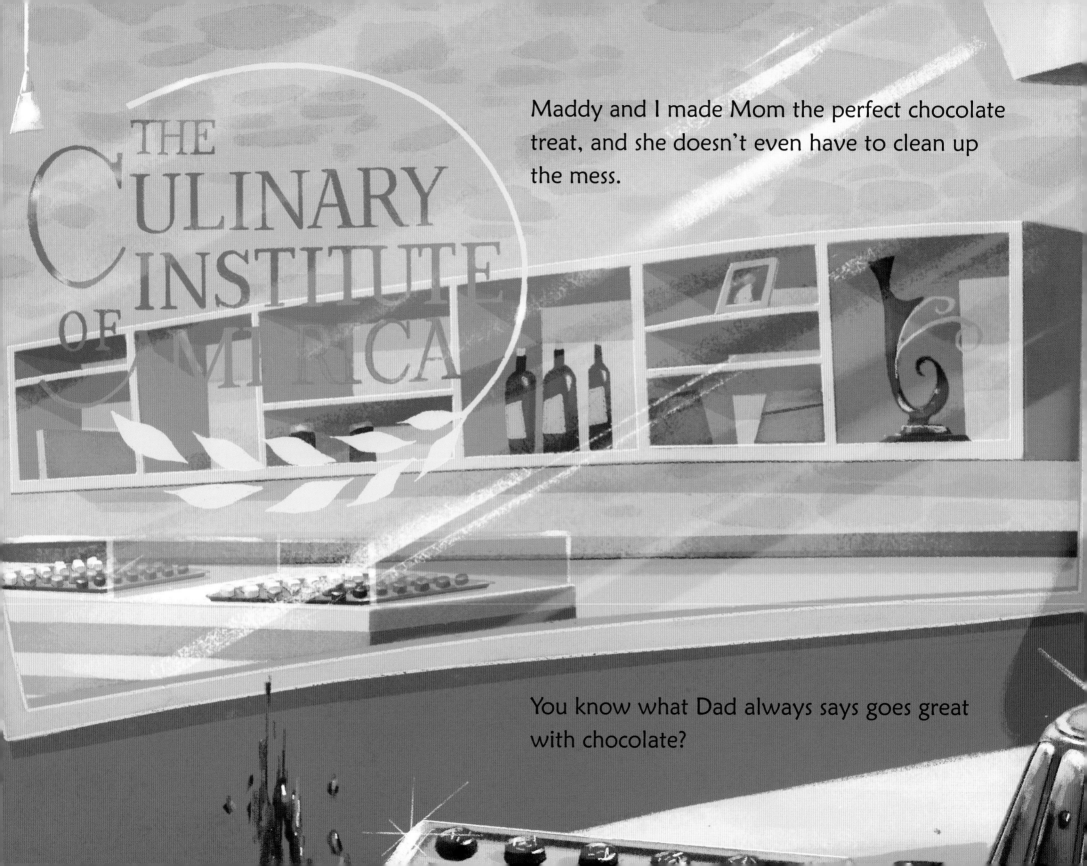

Maddy and I made Mom the perfect chocolate treat, and she doesn't even have to clean up the mess.

You know what Dad always says goes great with chocolate?

Wine. We do our best to stomp out every last bit of juice. I think this will be a fine vintage.

Our feet are exhausted. That limo
sure looks comfortable.

Now, this is the way to travel. Maddy opens the moon roof, I turn on some tunes, and we sing as loud as we can.

Maddy and I couldn't resist stopping for a mud bath. I thought a bath was to get rid of the mud! I find it very relaxing, and Maddy likes how the mud feels between her toes.

Napa has so many great adventures. I wonder what we should do tomorrow?

Thank you to Napa for providing a wonderful place to live and visit.
We would like to give a special "thank you" to the local businesses
that are featured and helped support our book.

Butter Cream Bakery & Diner
2297 Jefferson Street
Napa, CA 94559
(707) 255-6700
www.buttercreambakery.com

The Culinary Institute of America at Greystone
2555 Main Street
St. Helena, CA 94574
(707) 967-1100
www.ciachef.edu

Napa Valley Balloons, Inc.
301 Post Street
Napa, CA 94559
(800) 253-2224
www.napavalleyballoons.com

Napa Valley Wine Train
1275 McKinstry Street
Napa, CA 94559
(800) 427-4124
www.winetrain.com

Thank you to the businesses below who allowed us the opportunity to depict them in our children's book.

Oxbow Public Market
644 First Street
Napa, CA 94559
(707) 226-6529
www.oxbowpublicmarket.com

Gott's Roadside
644 First Street
Napa, CA 94559
(707) 224-6900
www.gotts.com

Winship Building
948 Main Street
Napa, CA 94559
(510) 529-2611

River Front Building
600 Main Street
Napa, CA 94559
(510) 529-2611